CAN YOU FIND IT?

Find It at the
BEACH

Dee Phillips

GARETH**STEVENS**
PUBLISHING
A Member of the WRC Media Family of Companies

D1153970

Please visit our web site at: www.garethstevens.com
For a free color catalog describing Gareth Stevens Publishing's list of high-quality books
and multimedia programs, call 1-800-542-2595 (USA) or 1-800-387-3178 (Canada).
Gareth Stevens Publishing's fax: (414) 332-3567.

Library of Congress Cataloging-in-Publication Data

Phillips, Dee, 1967-
    Find it at the beach / by Dee Phillips.
      p. cm. – (Can you find it?)
    ISBN 0-8368-6298-8 (lib. bdg.)
    1. Seashore animals–Juvenile literature. I. Title.
  QL122.2.P476   2006
  578.769'9–dc22   2005056345

This North American edition first published in 2006 by
Gareth Stevens Publishing
A Member of the WRC Media Family of Companies
330 West Olive Street, Suite 100
Milwaukee, WI 53212 USA

This U.S. edition copyright © 2006 by Gareth Stevens, Inc. Original edition copyright © 2005 by
ticktock Entertainment Ltd. First published in Great Britain in 2005 by ticktock Media Ltd., Unit 2,
Orchard Business Centre, North Farm Road, Tunbridge Wells, Kent TN2 3XF.

Gareth Stevens series editor: Dorothy L. Gibbs
Gareth Stevens graphic designer: Charlie Dahl
Gareth Stevens art direction: Tammy West

Picture credits: (t=top, b=bottom, l=left, r=right, c=center)
Ardea Images: 3, 7t. FLPA: 1, 4-5, 9, 13, 14-15c, 18br, 20-21b.
Every effort has been made to trace the copyright holders for the pictures used in this book.
We apologize in advance for any unintentional omissions and would be pleased to insert the
appropriate acknowledgements in any subsequent edition.

Printed in the United States of America

1 2 3 4 5 6 7 8 9 10 09 08 07 06

Words that appear in the glossary are printed in
boldface type the first time they occur in the text.

Contents

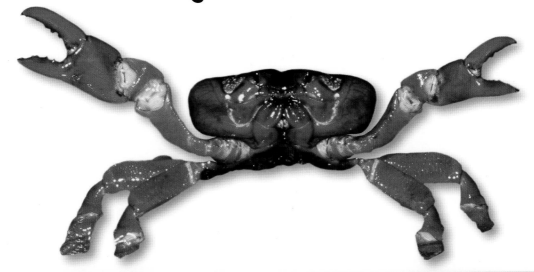

The Beach

There is so much to see at the beach, from seabirds soaring overhead to creatures **lurking** in **tide pools** or scurrying across the sand.

What can you find at the beach?

Crab

Seaweed

Seagull

Puffin

Starfish

Boat

Limpet shells

Seal

Driftwood

Crab

A crab is a crustacean, which is an animal that has a hard shell covering its soft body. There are about 4,500 different kinds of crabs. Most kinds live in water, but some kinds prefer sandy beaches.

Crabs have ten legs. They use their legs for both swimming and walking – but crabs only walk sideways!

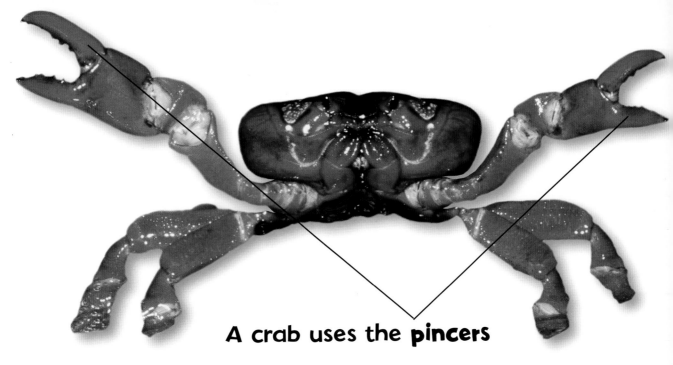

A crab uses the **pincers**

on its two front legs to catch food.

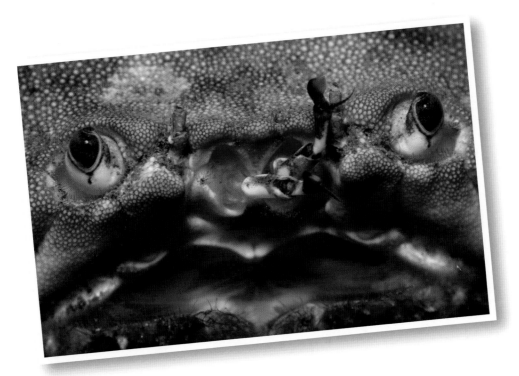

The largest crabs can be 12 feet (3.5 meters) across.

The smallest are only about the size of marbles.

Seaweed

Seaweed is a type of plant that grows in the ocean. It is found mainly in shallow water because it needs sunlight to live.

Because seaweed does not have roots, large clumps of it often wash up onto rocks and beaches.

There may be as many as six thousand different kinds of seaweeds. Some varieties just look brown and stringy, but others are very beautiful.

Seaweed is not a true plant. It is a form of **algae**.
Its leaves, which are called blades, are often green,
but they also may be red, blue, brown, or gold.

Seagull

Seagulls are large, noisy birds with powerful wings. They can be seen soaring over oceans and other large bodies of water almost everywhere in the world.

As they fly, seagulls are always on the lookout for food. They eat everything from fish and insects to scraps of garbage.

A seagull's sharp beak helps it catch and eat fish.

Most seagulls live in large groups called flocks.

The long, narrow wings of a seagull help it glide gracefully over the waves. Seagulls can swim, too!

Puffin

Puffins are easy to recognize. These **Arctic** seabirds have distinctive black and white **plumage**, brightly colored triangular beaks, and orange legs.

A puffin has webbed feet.

Puffins are very good swimmers. They dive deep under the water to catch the fish they like to eat.

A puffin's small wings are better for swimming than flying.

Starfish

Starfishes live in every ocean of the world. Different kinds of starfishes live in different kinds of places, from **tropical** seas to the icy Arctic.

Most starfish have five arms. The arms of a starfish are strong enough to open the **shellfish** they like to eat.

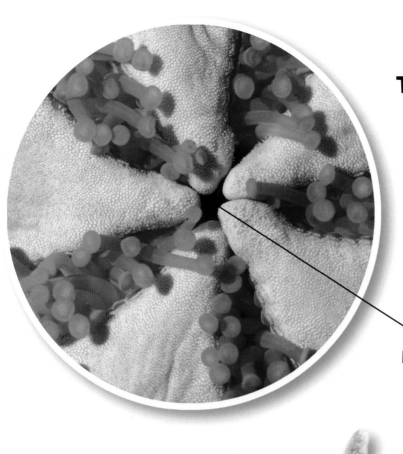

The mouth of a starfish is in the middle of its body.

mouth

suckers

On its underside, a starfish has **suckers** along each arm, which help it cling to rocks.

Boat

Boats of many kinds can be found along ocean coastlines. Some are used for fun. Others are for work.

Small boats can be used for fishing near shore.

Larger fishing boats can go out to deeper water. Workers on these boats use nets to catch fish.

Lifeboats are specially built so they are difficult to sink. These boats must be able to go out on rough seas to rescue people.

Limpet Shells

Pointed, hatlike shells found on rocky beaches protect the bodies of small sea animals called limpets.

Limpets eat algae, seaweed, and other ocean plants.

Under its shell, a limpet has one foot. The limpet moves by **rippling** its foot like a wave.

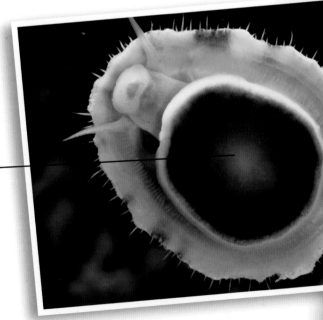

When it is not moving around, a limpet uses its foot like a suction cup to attach its body firmly to a rock.

Seal

Seals are ocean **mammals**. Some kinds of seals never leave the water, but others come to land to **breed**.

At the front of its body, a seal has **flippers** that help it move swiftly through the water.

Seals swim to the surface of the water to breathe air through their nostrils.

A seal has thick, waterproof fur. An adult seal can have as many as 800 million hairs on its body.

Thick fat called blubber also covers a seal's body. The blubber helps keep the seal warm.

Driftwood

Driftwood is the name for pieces of wood that float, or drift along, in the sea. The wood may be in the water for many years before it finally washes up onto the beach.

Driftwood may come from wrecked ships or from trees that were carried off by ocean tides.

Artists often collect driftwood from beaches and use it to make **sculptures.**

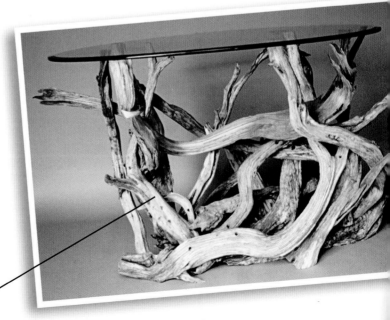

A piece of
driftwood may
travel thousands
of miles (kilometers) before
ocean waves carry it to shore.

Glossary

algae – tiny plants that have no roots, stems, or leaves and which float in water

arctic – from the region around the North Pole

breed – to produce young, or offspring

flippers – the paddlelike body parts on some animals that swim

lurking – waiting or hiding in a secret way

mammals – animals with backbones that give birth to live babies and feed their babies milk from the mother's body

pincers – claws made up of two sections that open and close

plumage – the feathers that cover a bird's body

rippling – moving with a wavelike motion

sculptures – works of art made by molding clay or carving wood or stone

shellfish – sea animals with soft bodies that are protected by shells

suckers – rounded objects that cling to surfaces by means of suction

tide pools – small pools of ocean water, plants, and animals that form on beaches when the tide goes out

tropical – from the warm regions of Earth that lie just to the north and south of the Equator